CHESTER'S

PIANO DUETS

VOLUME TWO
Written and Arranged by Carol Barratt

Dear Teacher,

These duets are intended for use in conjunction with the Chester Easiest Piano Course Book 3. In addition, by following each five-finger position indicated at the top of every page, they can be used by any beginner.

First and Second Player parts are of equal difficulty so that the pupil may become familiar with the entire piece.

The fun and invaluable experience of ensemble playing should be encouraged from the earliest days, and these duets are designed to develop a strong sense of rhythm, phrasing and dynamic shading.

Enjoy the music!

Carol Barratt

Chester Music Limited

GRASS SO GREEN
Second player

Play this page an octave lower than it is written.

Czech Folk Song

GRASS SO GREEN
First player

Play this page an octave higher than it is written.

Czech Folk Song

*Add a few claps to the first few bars e.g.

4

SPRING-HEEL-JACK
Second player

Play this page an octave lower than it is written.

Carol Barratt

SPRING-HEEL-JACK

First player

Play this page an octave higher than it is written.

Carol Barratt

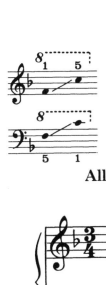

ALLEGRETTO
Second player

Watch out. Both hands are in the 𝄢:

From J. Hook
(1746-1827)

✻ 8........ This sign tells you to play the notes an octave lower than written.

ALLEGRETTO
First player

Watch out. Both hands are in the 𝄞

From J. Hook
(1746-1827)

8

From now on, specific
hand positions will not
necessarily be used.

LAVENDER'S BLUE
Second player

Traditional English

From now on, specific
hand positions will not
necessarily be used.

LAVENDER'S BLUE
First player

Traditional English

*8········ : **This sign tells you to play the notes an octave higher than written.**

WALTZ

Second player

From F. Schubert
(1797-1828)

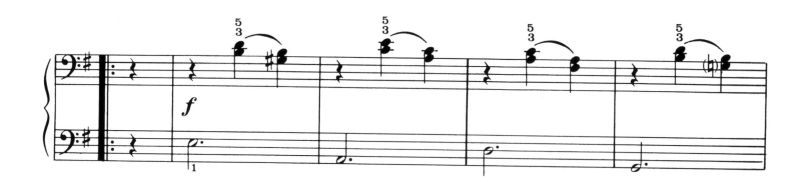

WALTZ

First player

Play this page an octave higher than it is written.

From F. Schubert
(1797-1828)

BUSKER BROWN
Second player

Carol Barratt

BUSKER BROWN

First player

Carol Barratt

*Whistle something suitable for four bars. Maybe starting with

14

Make sure you know these notes

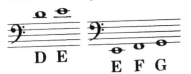

D E   E F G

SARABANDE

Second player

From J.P. Rameau
(1683-1764)

Andante

Make sure you know these notes

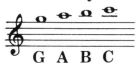

G A B C

SARABANDE

First player

From J.R. Rameau
(1683-1764)

SHE'LL BE COMING ROUND THE MOUNTAIN
Second player

Traditional American

SHE'LL BE COMING ROUND THE MOUNTAIN
First player

Traditional American

DURETTO

Second player

Attrib. O. Gibbons
(1583-1625)

DURETTO

First player

Attrib. O. Gibbons
(1583-1625)

BURLESQUE

(From a collection of pieces given to Wolfgang Mozart on his sixth birthday)

Second player

From L. Mozart
(1719-1787)

BURLESQUE

(From a collection of pieces given to Wolfgang Mozart on his sixth birthday)

First player

From L. Mozart
(1719-1787)

COOKHOUSE SHUFFLE

Second player

Carol Barratt

CHEERIO!

COOKHOUSE SHUFFLE

First player

Carol Barratt

CHEERIO!